Eating Fried Chicken With Moses

A Look Into Heaven

Pat Mallory

Copyright © 2014 by Pat Mallory

Eating Fried Chicken With Moses
A Look Into Heaven
by Pat Mallory

Printed in the United States of America

ISBN 9781498420624

All rights reserved solely by the author. The author guarantees all contents are original and do not infringe upon the legal rights of any other person or work. No part of this book may be reproduced in any form without the permission of the author. The views expressed in this book are not necessarily those of the publisher.

Scripture quotations taken from the King James Version (KJV) – *public domain*

www.xulonpress.com

"Eating Fried Chicken With Moses" is a book about Heaven. Jesus said in His Holy Word that when we all get to heaven we will feast at "the" Table. Now this says there won't be a Baptist table, a Methodist table, a head table, a servant's table, but we will all be at one table. Now I don't know about you, but that sounds exciting to me. Actually it is beyond my wildest imagination so I can just imagine as we are all at the table we may just want to ask the others at the table some questions. Some of my questions are in this book and I attempt to answer some questions that we somehow overlook as we study the Bible. We seem to always remember the mistakes and overlook the victories. My hope in writing this book is that we will get the whole picture and a new perspective so that we are ready to feast at "the" TABLE.

Pat is the Minister of Ministries and Missions at First Baptist Church in Tyler, Texas. Ordained into the ministry by the First Baptist Church in July, 1999. Pat has been active in several Texas churches in the areas of Women's Ministry, Singles Ministries, Senior Adult Ministry,

Evangelism, Internationals, Pastoral Care, Bible Study, Music and Motivational Speaking. Pat serves on the Advisory committee for Smith Baptist Association, the Texas Council for the Cooperative Baptist Fellowship, Missions Funding Committee for the BGCT, the Heath Foundation Board of Directors, Emeritus Board Member for Bethesda, Past President of Path, and serves as the Executive Director for the Gateway to Hope Day Resource Room for the homeless. Previous books include "Not On My Porch", Whoa, Man! See What God Did with a Rib", "A Godly Man! Who Can Find one?", "One Of Us Has Alzheimer's!", "I Hear My Father Calling...so What's a Girl to Do?", and "Into Each Life Some Rain Must Fall...But, God!". Pat's passion is serving God by helping others. She is the widow of Tommy G. Mallory. They have three children, Traci McFadden and husband, Ron, Trent Mallory and wife Becky (Crockett), Terrell Mallory and wife Melinda (Clark). They are also blessed with six grandchildren, Taylor and Tanner McFadden, Elizabeth, Todd, Mollie and Boston Mallory who all reside in the Metroplex area of Texas and are the greatest joy and achievement of Pat's life.

"EATING FRIED CHICKEN WITH MOSES"
By *Pat Mallory*

TABLE OF CONTENTS

Introduction Eating Fried Chicken with Moses ix

Chapter One Checking the Weather with Noah 15

Chapter Two Preparing for Battle with Joshua.......................19

Chapter Three Dealing with Hot Spots from Daniel........................25

Chapter Four Travel Planning With Elijah..................................33

Chapter Five Obedience from Jonah..........35

Chapter Six Patience from Job 39

Chapter Seven Mountain Climbing From Moses 45

Chapter Eight Dealing with Pride from Sampson 49

Chapter Nine Accepting Family from Joseph 55

Chapter Ten Sunbathing Tips from Bathsheba 59

INTRODUCTION

"EATING CHICKEN WITH MOSES"

Now when you see that title, you just may say..."how do you know Moses will be in Heaven", and even greater is the question..."What makes you think there will be fried chicken in Heaven???!! These are good questions we will address, but first, have you ever wondered why God created man in the first place??

One day we will know the answer to that question and all our questions, but, in the meantime, when that question crosses my mind...the answer that comes to me is God wanted someone to choose to love Him. He had all the angels in Heaven singing and praising Him, but...they had no choice. I have always wondered if when God created man in His image and gave him choices if that could not have been to have someone choose to love Him. Mankind, as a whole, beginning with Adam and Eve, almost always made the wrong choice. But, because God loves us, He continued to give them opportunity after opportunity to choose God. The Old Testament is filled with all the men and women who were made by God to bring mankind into a relationship with Him. Mankind tried to earn a relationship and failed every time. At the end of the Old Testament there was 400 years of silence from God and then He sent His Only Begotten Son, Jesus, to die for our sins and when man chose to believe, the love relationship between God and Man was secured by Grace from God and Through Faith in God by man.

"For by Grace are you saved through Faith!
"HALLELUJAH!

    Jesus is the bridge whereby man can choose to Love God and one day dwell with Him together forever reaping the Joy of Loved Shared!
    Mankind has so many questions and theories that will only be answered when those who choose Jesus can be at home with the Father. In the meantime, we have the Holy Spirit to guide and comfort us as we serve Him and follow His command to "Go into all the world, teaching everything Jesus taught, baptizing others in the name of the Father, the Son and The Holy Spirit."

We write books and songs and speculate on what home and heaven will be like, but…in the meantime we can never possibly grasp the magnitude of living forever with our Father in Heaven.

Bill and Gloria Gaither wrote and recorded the best guess I can imagine in their song "Jesus I heard You Had A Big House." Goes like this….

"Jesus, I heard You had a big house
where I'd have a room of my own,
and Jesus, I heard You had a big yard,
big enough to let a kid roam.
I heard you had clothes in your closet,
just the right size that I wear,
and Jesus, I heard if I'd give You my heart
that You would let me go there.

Jesus, I heard about mealtime
when all of Your children come to eat,
I heard You've got a great big table
where ev'ry kid can have a seat.
Jesus I heard there'd be plenty of
good things
for children to share,
and Jesus, I just want to tell You,
I sure would like to go there.
Jesus, I heard that in your big house
ther's plenty of love to go 'round;
I heard ther's always singing and laughter

to fill the place with happy sounds.
And I've been thinking that a friend
who'd planned to give me all that He's got
before I had even met Him,
Well, He sure must love me a lot!
Yes, He sure must love me a lot!"

So, who do you think we will live in the Big House with?,, Adam, Eve, Cain, Abel, and Seth. Grandma, Mamma, Daddy?

Jesus is recorded in John 14 to have told His followers at His translation, "I go to prepare a place for you and If I go, I will come again so that where I am, You will be also. He has even said we will "feast at His Table!" In Luke 22:30 Jesus says we will "drink at My Table in My Kingdom." He tells us we will know as we are known, and in John 14:2, Jesus says "In my Father's House are many Mansions...."

WE really won't know what Heaven is like until we are there, but one thing is sure...It will be more than we can possibly imagine, so in writing this we are limited to words and circumstances we can relate to so while there may not really be "chicken " or whatever, those phrases represent in heaven, but for this book, "chicken", represents the best we can imagine!

Also "chicken" is not the point. Being at home with Jesus and all those who have gone before us and having the privilege to sit at His table with all believers and listen to the testimonies. Moses can tell us all about his many adventures following God's directions and there is nothing better than to hear it from the people who lived it. I want to ask Moses "What made you decide to lead

God's people out of bondage?' I have read that his first answer to God was "Send my Brother."

As to how we know Moses will be there is, that he, like all us, is there because of his faith and Jesus sacrifice. A lot of folks wonder how those who believed before Jesus came to earth and died for our sins can be saved. Let's just say salvation is through faith by grace and that grace can be retroactive. God doesn't count time the way mankind does. He looks at the heart and our actions. God knows who is faithful and recognizes those who are just saying words. Actions always speak louder than words.

Moses walked the walk and climbed many a mountain because God told him too. He got the people to the promised land, but did not get to go in because God had a better plan. He was taken up into Heaven (the real promised land Deut. 34:5-6) and got the scenic view of the whole land and God's personal tour. Now it can't get any better than that. Moses was and is there with God in the eternal promised land!!

In fact, he and Elijah, who did not die, but was taken up in a whirlwind (II Kings 2:11) came down from heaven to be with Jesus when he was taken home at His transfiguration recorded in Matthew 17:1-3 "After six days Jesus took with him Peter, James and John the brother of James, and led them up a high mountain by themselves. There he was transfigured before them. His face shone like the sun and his clothes became as white as the light. (2 Peter 1:16-18) Just then, there appeared before them, Moses and Elijah, talking with Jesus

CHAPTER ONE

"CHECKING THE WEATHER WITH NOAH"

I really want to get to sit next to Noah one day at God's table because I just want to hear from his lips how he had such a strong faith in God! Wow! If a man ever lived with more faith I can't imagine...God told Noah there was going to be a flood and that he was to build an ark (Genesis 6:9- 9:29) that would hold "seven of every kind of clean animal, male and it's mate, and two of every kind of unclean animal, a male and its mate, and also seven of every kind of bird, male and female, to keep their various kinds alive throughout the earth." Then God gave Noah the specifics of the ark which were seemingly impossible in my mind, but Noah found Grace in the eyes of the Lord and "Whoa!"

It seems when one finds grace in the eyes of the Lord, He is also given a task to perform. I think of all the doors God has opened for me that I found too big a task, then I look at Noah. First the task of building the ark to God's specifications looks impossible to mankind, but... Noah just went to work and worked for 120 years finding the materials, assembly them and putting them together while all around him everyone was making fun of his faith. Can't you just hear them saying things like "ole Noah" must be crazy....look at what he is doing because he thinks it's going to come a flood. Just think years went by and Noah remains at his task, believing God. Not just in God, but what God said to him.

I wonder what God could do through each of us, if we believed what He has said and is saying to each of us on a daily basis. Most of us would say, after a couple of days, "I must have misunderstood..." and moved on to one of our personal projects. It just blows my mind that any human would be as believing and faithful as Noah. I want to ask him about how he could be so strong.

Then there was the task of gathering up two of all the living creatures, plus his family, not knowing how long they would be in the ark. Now I don't know about you, but most folks I know have a little trouble being locked up anywhere for any time with family. But Noah! I want to tell him how much I admire his faith, his stamina, his patience and let him know I understand when one of the first things he did on stepping on Mount Ararat was planting a vineyard and then becoming drunk on some of its wine causing him shame before his son, Ham. We need to remember that the first thing he did was build an altar to God. Isn't it just atypical that we focus on the frailties of one another, rather than the good stuff?

Ham ran and told his brothers, but Shem and Japheth took a garment and laid it across their shoulders, then they walked in backward and covered their father's nakedness. Their faces were turned the other way so that they would not see their father's nakedness. When Noah awoke and discovered who had done what, he cursed Canaan, the son of Ham and blessed Shem and Japheth. Noah lived for 350 more years and died having lived a total of 950 years on this earth. Do the math! Think how old Noah was when he started his greatest act of obedience to God's command.

I want to ask Noah some questions, like did you ever just want to give up? Did you ever just think maybe I misunderstood what God said? Did you ever ask "Why me, Lord?" I want to ask these questions because I stand in awe at the strength, faithfulness, and integrity of Noah and pray daily for just a smathering of Noah's walk with God. How long has it been since you had a little talk with God?

CHAPTER Two

PREPARING FOR BATTLE WITH JOSHUA

One has to wonder what he was thinking. Forty years before he was standing there As we look at Joshua standing before the Jordan River for the second time, one because Moses had sent him and Caleb to spy out the land as God had told him to do. They went back and gave a good report, but the people...is that not a familiar phrase? The land was filled with good things, but the people chose to see the problems rather than focus on the good. It seems we have not learned a lot since those days of old.

Now the first time the people chose to turn back and could not be convinced that they could trust God to give them victory over the enemy, and Joshua is once again trying to convince the people. Moses has died and now Joshua is the leader. He follows Moses example and sends two spies into the land to scope it out. They entered the city and met a woman named Rahab, who was a prostitute, who probably also ran an inn. She hid the spies on the roof of her house and when the soldiers from the city came she told them that the men had left before the closing of the gates and that they needed to hurry and catch them. Rahab then went to the spies and told them what she and the people of the city knew about Joshua and his army. The people were terrified because they knew that God had promised the land to the children of Israel.

Because of Rahab's courage and kindness the spies promised her that she and her family would be spared. She was to hang a scarlet thread out her window so that the Israelites would know which commitment. house was hers so that her family would be spared.

Joshua divided the people into three groups. The priests, one man from each tribe and the rest of Israel. The priests carried the Ark of the Covenant and stepped into the river which opened up to one side and dried up to the other. The people of Israel crossed over on dry land. Now this was not their first dry land experience. But because the first time did not seem to have been remembered in the bad days, twelve men picked up a boulder from the dry riverbed and carried it out. These twelve stones were placed in the

Promised Land as a reminder to future generations of how God lead Israel out of the wilderness into the land of promise. We still need extra reminders of all the good things God has done each time we face a new trial.

Well things were looking good in their new land and then Joshua got a surprise visit from God. He was deep in thought looking at the city of Jericho when a man appeared before him with a drawn sword. Joshua asked a simple question, but got a confusing answer. Joshua asked, "Are you for us or against us?" The answer was the one standing before him was the captain of the Lord's host and Joshua needed to decide the answer to his own question...was Joshua and Israel on God's side or with the enemy? Have you ever stood where Joshua stood and did you recognize that it was God testing your Joshua answered wisely by bowing before the Lord. He then pledged his allegiance to the Lord and removed his shoes as instructed and worshiped God on Holy Ground. Makes one wonder if every time we come to a cross road in life, do we remember that as believers we are on Holy Ground and we need to take off our shoes (or our way) and bow before the Lord.

Then Joshua was given the battle plan. They were to march around Jericho every day for six days. The priests were to go behind then blowing seven trumpets of ram's horns before the Ark. Then on the seventh day the host was to compass the city seven times while the priests blew their trumpets. At the completion of the seventh time they were to make a long loud blast with their trumpets and all the people were to shout.

One can only imagine what was going in the soldiers minds, but they obeyed and the walls came tumbling down.

Rahab and her family were able to receive grace as the soldiers fulfilled their promise to her. Because of her faith in God she is mentioned several times and became an ancestor to King David and Jesus Christ.

So we have this experience of Joshua to look at the crossing of the Jordan River as salvation and the occupying of the land as a victorious Christian life. If you believe… you will receive. How often do we think we have a better plan, or try to alter the plans of God because we think we know better. I wonder is God at this very moment guiding you to step into the water so He can dry up the floods in your life and then give a victory march around your "city". Too often we toot our own horns, instead of following God's direction. I challenge you to follow God's plan and then testify to the "walls" that come tumbling down in your life. Sing with me…. "Joshua fought the battle of Jericho,

Jericho, Jericho. Joshua fought the battle of Jericho and the walls came tumbling down."

CHAPTER THREE

GETTING OUT OF HOT SPOTS WITH DANIEL

Does the phrase "Out of the frying pan, into the fire" describe your life? Well it sure could describe the life of Daniel! It always seems like when you are in God's favor Satan enters the scene! We read in the Bible where God gave wisdom to Daniel and then all hell broke loose. Nebuchadnezzar took control and ordered that special young men of the Israelites without any defect, handsome, showing aptitude for every kind of learning, well informed, quick to understand and qualified to serve in the king's palace be taught the language and literature of the Babylonians. The king assigned them a daily amount of food and wine from the king's table. They were to be trained for three years and after that they were to enter into the king's service. But Daniel...refused to defile himself. Then God! There is a lesson here. Pay attention! God caused the official to show favor and sympathy to Daniel, but he was fearful for his own life if these young men should start looking worse than the other young men of their age.

Some of the young men from Judah with Daniel were Hananiah, Mishael and Azariah. The official gave them new names: To Daniel, the name Belteshazzar; to Hannaniah, Shadrach; to Mishael, Meshach; and to Azariah, Abednego. After hearing the concern of the official over them Daniel offered him a deal, "Please test your servants for ten days: Give us nothing but vegetable to eat and water to drink. Then compare our appearance with that of the young men who eat the royal food then treat your servant in accordance with what you see. The official agreed. At the end of the ten days these men looked healthier and better nourished than any of the young men who ate the royal food, so the guard took away their choice foods and the wine and they were to drink only water and gave them vegetables instead. But God gave these four young men knowledge and understanding of all kinds of literature and learning and Daniel could understand visions and dreams of all kinds. And then the adventure was on. I am always amazed at with God's gifts there always comes an assignment. As I look back over my life, there is a pattern of a God blessing followed by a God assignment. Gives new meaning to "be careful what you ask for".

Well, sure enough, King Nebuchadnezzar had a dream and guess who got to interpret that dream...right, Daniel! Actually he volunteered to do the interpreting to save the lives of the wise men who were unable to interpret the dream. When the king asked if he could interpret the dream, Daniel's reply is classic and a real lesson for us. Daniel replied "No wise man, enchanter, magician or diviner can explain to the king the mystery he has asked about, but there is a God in heaven who reveals mysteries. He has shown King Nebuchadnezzar what will happen in the days to come. Daniel continued to reveal that God had shown the king what would happen in days to come and then the revealer of mysteries showed you what is going to happen, As for me this mystery has been revealed to me, not because I have greater wisdom than other living men, but so that you, O king, may know the interpretation and that you may understand what went through your mind.

The king was please and promoted Daniel and his friends to a higher position and lavished gifts upon Daniel. He began to build a statue for the people to worship and issued a decree that anyone who did not fall down and worship at the sound of the trumpet would be thrown into the fire of the furnace.

Daniels' friends refused to worship anything other than God.

The king became very angry and ordered them to be cast into the furnace, Shadrach, Meshach and Abednego responded with a strong faith, that their God is able to save us from it and even if he does not we want you to know, O king, that we will not serve your gods or worship the image of gold you have set up. Now the king was furious and order the furnace to be heated up seven times hotter than usual and commanded the three friends of Daniel be cast into the blazing furnace which was so hot that the flames of the fire killed the soldiers who threw the three friends of Daniel into the flaming furnace. Then the king leaped to his feet and asked, "Weren't there three men thrown into the furnace??" "Certainly", came the reply from the kings advisors" "The why do I see four!!" cried the king, why the fourth one looks like a son of God." He then opened the furnace and shouted "Shadrach, Meshach and Abednego, servants of the Most High God, come out! Come Here!" All were amazed because they say that the fire had not harmed their bodies nor was a hair of their heads singed; their robes were not scorched, and there was no smell of fire on them. Then Nebuchadnezzar said, "Praise be to the God of Shadrach, Meshach and Abednego, who has sent his angel and rescued his servants:

They trusted in him and defied the king's command and were willing to give up their lives rather than serve or worship any god except their own God!" Then he issued a decree that the people of any nation or language who say anything against the God of Shadrach, Meshach and Abednego be cut into pieces and their houses be turned into piles of rubble , FOR NO OTHER GOD CAN SAVE IN THIS WAY!" Wow! Why are we still so small in our faith?

Well this was just the beginning of one dream and interpretation after another. The king dreamed about a tree, Daniel interprets the dream. The dream is fulfilled and all this culminates with Nebuchadnezzar giving praises and exalting and glorifying the King of heaven, because "everything he does is right and all his ways are just and those who walk in pride he is able to humble."

Next came the dream of the writing on the wall and Daniel's interpretation of that writing which culminated with Daniel being thrown into the Lion's den. It seems the king's wisemen were unable to interpret the writing so the king went to Daniel and offered to clothe Daniel in purple and have a gold chain placed around his neck and was going to make Daniel third in the chain of command in the kingdom. Daniel's reply is classic. He basically said, keep all your "stuff", but I will interpret the writing.

Daniel started with the details of what had happened to Nebuchadnezzar because he became arrogant and hardened with pride which resulted in his being deposed from the royal throne and stripped of his glory. He was driven away from people and given the mind of an animal. He lived like a donkey and ate grass like cattle; his body was drenched with the dew of heaven, until he acknowledged the Most High God is sovereign over the kingdoms of men and sets over them anyone He pleases.

Next Daniel addressed Belshazzar that as the son of Nebuchadnezzar he had not humbled himself even though he knew all of this he had set himself up against the God of Heaven. As a result he received the message from God that his days were numbered and that his reign would end. He had been weighed on the scales and was found wanting. His kingdom would be divided and given to the Medes and the Persians.

Belshazzar still had Daniel clothed in purple and a gold chain was placed around his neck. He was proclaimed to be the third highest ruler in the kingdom. That very night Belshazzar, king of the Babylonians was slain and Darius, the Mede took over the kingdom.

Next Daniel is thrown into the lion's den… because he openly disobeyed the decree of King Darius by opening his window and praying to his God...but God closed the mouths of the lions! The end result was those who had accused Daniel were thrown into the lion's den. Then King Darius decreed that everyone was to worship the God of Daniel! Then Daniel has the dream of the four beasts...a lion, a bear, a leopard and a the beast with ten horns followed by a vision of one like the Son of God, The Ancient of Days which were interpreted as the kingdoms that would arise upon the earth until the kingdom of the most High, which will have no end. Next Daniel had a vision of a ram and a goat which was interpreted by the angel, Gabriel as a vision of the end of time, which appalled Daniel because, as he said, "it is beyond understanding".

So Daniel turned to the Lord and pleaded with Him in prayer and petition in fasting, and in sackcloth and ashes. He prayed:

"O Lord, the great and awesome God, who keeps his covenant of love with all who obey Him and keep His command...(see Daniel 9:4-19) While he was praying and confessing his sins Gabriel appeared and gave him the decree of the Seventy "sevens" followed by all the end of time prophecies concerning the times of distress and deliverance and concludes with the ultimate promise..."As for you go your way till the end. You will rest, and then at the end of the days you will rise to receive your allotted inheritance." Now that's what I'm talking about!! I can't even imagine having this much knowledge and not being totally overwhelmed and yet... isn't that exactly where we are as believers? We who accept the King of Kings have the promise...,we will rise!!

And not just rise, but sit at the table with Daniel too. I can't wait to meet this ultimate man of faith to whom God revealed his plans for the future and the hereafter!!

Anytime you think you are having a bad day...remember Daniel and see the victory!

CHAPTER FOUR

TRAVEL PLANNING WITH ELIJAH

Elijah was a prophet who predicted famine in Israel, was fed by ravens, raised Sidonian widow's son, defeated the prophets of Baal at Carmel, ran from Jezabel, was taken to heaven in a whirlwind, his return is prophesied. He is equated with John the Baptist. He appeared with Moses at the transfiguration of Jesus!! Wow!! Now there is a man on the move. I want to sit next to him at the Lord's table and get some insite and details as to what it was like to used in such a mighty way by our Lord!! His story is recorded in scripture in I and II Kings, Malachi and in the New Testament in the book of Matthew.

As we look his track record, it is interesting that maybe the wisest thing he ever did was to run from Jezabel! Seriously, how many times has the fall of a man been associated with an evil woman? I often warn men when they see cleavage at either end of a woman to run...it is a trap. Now we don't know if Jezabel showed cleavage, but she took some good men down, but..not Elijah! He ran and then was able to book a whirlwind to go home and then was given the honor of escorting Jesus home after His resurrection as a co-escort with Moses!

I want to ask him what was going through his mind as he was taken up in a whirlwind... did he know what was going on...was he afraid. Did he ask why me when chosen to be an escort for Jesus!! Talk about places of honor!!

CHAPTER FIVE

LEARNING OBEDIENCE FROM JONAH

Jonah was an Old Testament Prophet. Now a prophet is someone who speaks God's message to others. Jonah, like a lot of us, seemed to want to make the decisions as to whom he shared God's message. God had told him to go to Nineveh, but Jonah. I wonder how many times God has given us direction and we have had a "but, Jonah" response. You see Jonah did not like the people of Nineveh so he did not want them to be a part of God's provision. So he ran in the opposite direction and boarded a ship and headed to

Tarshish. This is always a mistake, because just as we have, "but, me", moments God shows us a "But, God" moment. In the case of Jonah, this stirred up a storm.

I love the way God always uses circumstances and other people to make a point. Now in the case of Jonah, the others on the boat wondered why the storm. They were shown that having Jonah on the boat was the problem and in typical human fashion, threw the "problem" overboard. There is a lesson here. What others so often see as a problem, God chooses to use to His glory. God had a big fish ready to pick up Jonah and deliver him to where God had planned for him to be, Nineveh. Can you even start to imagine being alive in the belly of a big fish and then vomited up in the very place you were attempting to avoid? Now this is what God calls an attitude adjustment. Ever needed one of those? Most of us understand this...When God has a plan, He works His plan. If you don't want to be in the belly of a big fish or worse, listen to the still small voice of God and go where He leads, Say what He has given you to say and make no detours.

Jonah finally recognized God's will, prayed and obediently went to preach the Word in Nineveh. The people believed and God had mercy on them and did not destroy them. Scripture then tells us God's decision, angered Jonah. He even reminded God that this was why he did not want to come to Nineveh. He knew of the Lord's grace and compassion, that he was slow to anger and abounding in love. A God who relents from sending calamity. So Jonah asks God to take away his life for he felt it would be better for him to die than to live. But God, said, "Have you any right to be angry?"

Now God had a lesson for Jonah and for you and me. Jonah went out and sat down at a place east of the city and made himself a shelter and sat in it's shade and waited to see what would happen to the city. Then the Lord God provided a vine and made it grow up over Jonah to give shade for his head to ease his discomfort, this made Jonah very happy. But at dawn the next day, God provided a worm, to chew the vine so that it withered. When the sun rose and provided a scorching east wind, and the sun blazed on Jonah's head so that he grew faint, he said "it would be better for me to die than to live." God asked him, "Do you have the right to be angry about the vine?

When Jonah answered, "I do", the Lord said, "you have been concerned about this vine, though you did not tend it or make it grow, it sprang up overnight and died overnight, But, NINEVEH has more than a hundred thousand people who cannot tell their right hand from their left and many cattle as well. Should I not be concerned about that great city?"

Basically, this message is "Get your priorities straight!!" We too often major on the minors when God has work for us to do. It is not up to us to choose to whom we share God's love, but to be obedient to God's command that we love one another. Red, yellow, black and white; rich, poor, homeless; obedient or those wandering in darkness. God's command is for us to go and bring all His children home!! How much plainer can this point be made than is recorded in God's word,

Jesus. Himself lived out this as He walked upon earth's sod, He always went where the need was the greatest. The adulterous woman, the woman at the well, the thief on the cross, those who crucified Jesus, all were recipients of His Amazing Grace!! Jesus said, "Father, forgive them, they know not what they do." Jesus said, "Where are your accusers?" Jesus said, "Today, you will be with me in paradise." Not once did Jesus say, When you get it together, or if you, He always said, "Come unto me all ye who are weary and I will give you rest." Come on… Can we afford to do any less…Let's agree to give to others what has been given to us! Amen!

CHAPTER SIX

LEARNING PATIENCE FROM JOB

Have you ever asked the question, "Why Me, Lord?" Most of us have because we have bought into the mentality that we should get what we deserve. Personally, I hope I never get what I deserve, I am more interested in God's Grace. Job is a good example in the Bible to show us that nothing passes to us or through us that has not been through the hands of God. If we are having "bad" times then God has a reason for a season.

It may be to teach us a lesson, so we can understand others pain, or it may be to show us the power of God and where we should place our trust and commitment.

Back in the days of Abraham, there lived a man named Job. Job was one of the wealthiest men on the face of the earth. He feared God and lived an upright life during the ancient patriarch period in the land of Uz a region of northern Arabia. His life answers the question as to why the righteous suffer. Now if a man ever had patience, that man was Job. He had patience in life's disasters, with his precious wife, and all of his "friends".

Now his story begins as he was going about his usual routine when one day the angels came to present themselves before the Lord and Satan came with them. Now we need to remember that Satan was once one of the angels, but was cast down for his desire to run things. So when he showed up with the angels, God asked where he came from...Satan replied, "From roaming through the earth and going back and forth in it." Then the Lord asks "Have you considered my servant Job? there is no one on earth like him: He is blameless and upright; a man who fears God and shuns evil." Now let's pause here a moment to reflect on God's assessment of Job. We need to keep this in mind as we look at the "rest of the story". Makes one wonder what God would say if one of us was the topic of a conversation between God and Satan. Satan's reply to God was something like "Yeah, Right! Look at the hedge of protection you have put around him. Take it down and he will surely curse You to your face!"

And the Lord said, "Very well, then everything he has is in your hands, BUT, on the man

Learning Patience From Job

himself, do not lay a finger!" So Job lost everything; his children, his servants, his sheep... everything except his wife and "friends". Now let's look at Job's reaction...He got up, tore his robe and shaved his head, then he fell on his knees and worshipped God!! He said, "Naked I came from my Mother's womb and naked I will depart. The Lord Gave and the Lord taketh away,. Blessed be the name of the Lord and be praised!" Yet in this Job did not sin by blaming God! Whoa! Now that is a Godly Man!

So Satan again asks permission to touch Job physically. God grants permission with the stipulation to spare Job's life.

Looks like God is in control to me...

So Job is covered with sores and as Job is scraping his sores, his wife, precious as she could be, speaks to Job, "Why don't you just curse God and die!" Now wasn't that special? Job's reply was "You are talking like a foolish woman, shall we accept good from God and not trouble?" Now his man knew about faith and patience, sounds like he just might have had a personal relationship with God.

Next Job's friends come to "comfort" him. God protect us from "comforting" friends who comfort as Job's friends. This results in Job cursing the day of his birth. Then for the longest time Job's "friends" remind him that he needs to confess "his sins" because God doesn't punish the innocent so he certainly must have sinned so...confess! Job then defends his integrity and expresses his desire to die. His friends, remind him that God is totally just, to which Job replies, "God destroys the blameless and the wicked... even if I am innocent, I cannot lift my head for I am full of shame." So, another "friend" tells Job that God is justified in His dealings." This same dialog goes on and on until finally Job states, "I know that my Redeemer lives and that in the end He will stand upon the earth!" "When I am tested I will come forth as gold!"

Next Job longs for the blessed days gone by and repents in dust and ashes and then prays for his "friends"! Now wait a minute that is a righteous man!! The Lord then restores and doubles his possessions and family. Job, then lived 140 years and saw his children and their children to the 4th generation and he died old and full of years!" Now that's what I am talking about..

Lessons to be learned from Job are:

1. Satan cannot bring destruction upon us without God's permissive will and God sets the limits.

Sometimes suffering is allowed to purify, to test, to teach or to strengthen our souls by showing us that when we feel we have lost all and only God remains, God is enough! God deserves and requests our love and praise regardless of our lot in life.

   2. God will deliver all suffering believers either in this life or the life to come! Thank You Jesus!

CHAPTER SEVEN

MOUNTAIN CLIMBING WITH MOSES

One can hear folks complaining that they are always in the valley and never get to the top of the mountain in life. Well maybe we just don't recognize the mountains. Moses spent a lot of time on mountain tops working or the Lord. Now what we mean when we talk about the top of the mountain is "easy street" where we are catered to and everything goes our way. We learn from Moses that "the top of the mountain" is not always easy. We learn that getting to the top is filled with difficult tasks and obedience to our Lord.

Now Moses was the son of Amram from the Levite tribe of Israel. He was a part of the second generation of Israelites born in Egypt. His parents were Jacob and Jochebed. He had a brother Aaron who was three years older and a sister Miriam that was seven years older. Now about the time of his birth the Pharoah commanded that all male Hebrew children be drowned in the Nile River...but, God had other plans for Moses.

Now while his mother was obedient and placed him in a basket in the Nile River, she did the motherly thing and had her daughter Miriam watch the basket to see what happened. Now as "luck" would have it or as ordained by God, the Pharoah's daughter came down to the river to bathe along with her attendants. When she saw the basket, she sent her attendants to bring it to her. When she saw the baby crying she felt sorry for him and said, "This must be one of the Hebrew children..." Miriam seized this opportunity to approach the Pharoah's daughter and offer to go get a Hebrew woman to nurse the baby. The Pharoah's daughter said yes... so guess where she took the baby.. to his mother, Jocabed. The princess even paid her to take care of him. Now when he was older, his mother brought him back to the princess who adopted him and named him Moses because she "lifted him out of the water." Remember that his mother at this point was willing to leave her child in God's hands and that is about as high on the mountain as one can get!!

Many years later Moses went to visit his own people, the Hebrews, he was appalled at how they were being treated and sort of took the matter into his own hands by killing the Egyptian taskmaster. Then he buried him in the sand to cover up his violent deed... which would come back to haunt him as our "cover ups" always do. He was to learn that when we hide our mistakes they always come back to haunt us so we need to learn to face our mistakes and put them to rest once and for all. Thus began the process of God restoring His people and getting them to the promised land through Moses. The promise was wonderful but the difficulty of the process could not be underestimated. Part of the process was God using Moses to tell the Egyptians God's plan of seven plagues coming if they did not let his people go. Israel then celebrated their first Passover and took their Exodus from Egypt. Now God had them take a wilderness detour as they were being pursued by the Egyptians then He parted the Red Sea and took them across to dry land where he later had Moses to strike the rock to provide them water to drink.

Two months after the Israelites left Egypt God revealed himself to Moses on Mt. Sinai and it was here that Moses received the Ten Commandments from God, followed by Israel accepting the Lord's Covenent and the completion of the Tabernacle. After wandering in the wilderness for 38 years they reached the land of Canaan. This is where they were divided into the Twelve Tribes of Israel who were asked to scout out the land resulting in the people rebelling against Moses and Aaron. Now because Moses and Aaron had not shown the Lord's Holiness they were not permitted to enter the Promised Land...but were taken hone to the "real" promised land where Moses, along with Elijah got to come down from Heaven to escort Jesus back to Heaven at His translation. Now that is what I call Blessed beyond measure. Now Moses has climbed the Highest Mountain. Higher than Mt. Nebo or Horeb where he had his burning Bush Experience.

CHAPTER EIGHT

DEALING WITH PRIDE FROM SAMPSON

Sampson was the strongest man who ever lived. His one weakness was women... and so the story goes on and on to the present...all of us can testify to that same weakness. It has brought down many a good man and woman.,, I try to warn both sexes that if you see or show cleavage at either end, RUN!!!

We can find Sampson's story in the book of Judges beginning in chapter eleven. Once again the Israelites did evil in the sight of the Lord so he had handed them over to the Philistines who had oppressed them for forty years. Sampson's father was named Manoah. He was from the tribe of Zorah and his wife was unable to become pregnant. Then an angel of the Lord appeared to her and said "Even though you have been unable to have children you will soon become pregnant and give birth to a son. So, be careful, you must not drink wine or any other alcoholic drink nor eat any forbidden food. You will soon become pregnant and give birth to a son, and his hair must never be cut. For he will be dedicated to God as a Nazarite from birth. He will begin to rescue Israel from the Philistines. Well immediately she went to tell her husband! Manoah prayed to the Lord saying, "LORD, please let the man of God come back and give us more instructions!" Now I can understand that request...I have often asked God to explain what is going on and never once has it been as shocking as this situation. But God answered Manoah's prayer...again to his wife...who ran immediately to find her husband and say "the man who appeared to me the other day is here again!!" Manoah immediately ran back and questioned the man. Now Manoah did not realize that it was not a man, but an angel. It was awhile before he realized this and then he told his wife,..they were surely going to die because they had seen God! His wife responded that if God was going to kill them, he surely would not have provided this wonderful miracle of a son. Soon the son was born and his mother named him Sampson, and the Lord blessed him as he grew up.

And then......the harmones took over!!! Samson saw a Philistine girl he wanted. Now who is surprised by this development?? He went to his parents and basically said "Get her for me!" His parents objected and reminded Samson that she was one of the enemy...to which he replied, I want her, get her for me. So the wedding was arranged, the wedding day arrived, but as they are on their way a young lion attacked Sampson but as he was attacked the Lord also came upon him and he ripped the lions' jaws apart with his bare hands.

He did not tell anyone about this and later when he returned for the wedding he turned off the path to look at the carcass of the lion. He found a swarm of bees had made some honey in the carcass. He ate some and gave some to his parents to eat and then he made up a riddle. "What is sweeter than honey? What is stronger than a lion?" Then he made a deal with the young men chosen to be his attendants. Basically, if they could solve the riddle then he would buy them thirty fine linen robes and thirty sets of festive clothing. If they could not solve the riddle, then they would purchase the same for Samson. Well the young men could not solve the riddle so they went to see his wife and threatened to burn her parent's house unless she could give them the answer. Here's where the plot thickens.

His wife began to cry and say he didn't love her, if he did he would not keep secrets. So, of course Samson told her, she told the young men who immediately flaunted their success in Sampson's face. I love Samson's response to the men. He said, "If you hadn't plowed with my heifer, you wouldn't have solved my riddle!!" Then the spirit of the Lord came upon him and is wife was given to the best man. Sampson later went to reclaim his wife and lost it when he discovered she had been given to the best man. Then Samson began to rack havoc on the Philistines. He killed 30 men that day and then killed 1,000 Philistines with the jawbone of an ass, carried off the Gates of Gaza, falls in love with Delilah who betrays him by revealing that his strength was in his hair and pushed down the temple of Dagon.

But now let us look at how God uses our mistakes. He never wastes a pain. We just have to surrender to His will. While it looks like things were running amuck for Samson, look at how God was defeating the enemy. After Delilah lulls Samson to sleep and cuts his hair, she yells "the Philistines are here!!" Samson attempts to brush himself off and realizes his strength is gone. The Philistines capture him, gouge out his eyes, and place him in prison...but then, his hair began to grow. His final victory came when he was taken to the temple so he could be mocked by the Philistines and that is when he brought the house down, killing more people when he died than while he was alive. Samson had judged Israel for twenty years and was laid to rest between his parents. Now I have got some tough questions for this man while we are feasting at THE TABLE!!

CHAPTER NINE

ACCEPTING FAMILY FROM JOSEPH

When we think of Joseph, we generally get hung up on the fact that he had a "coat of many colors". There is more to the story of Joseph than a gift from his father. First he was the eleventh son of Jacob and the first son of Rachel. While his father did gift him with a coat of many colors, it was his bragging about it that caused the most trouble. His over confidence lived up to the rule that over-confidence is usually viewed as a negative personality trait. Then to top the gift off was his telling his brothers, "that someday they and others would bow down to him. This coupled with the father's favoritism led to his brothers jealousy and the broken family relationships. In the end his brothers sold him into slavery and cut him off from his family altogether.

But, God!! Through years of difficulties and suffering, Joseph's overconfidence was transformed by God into a mature self-assurance. In times of personal struggle, this self-assurance, along with his personal knowledge of God, enabled Joseph to ask, "What shall I do now?" instead of "Why me, Lord?"

This is a life lesson, LEARN IT!

Joseph's self-assurance made him capable of tackling and succeeding at jobs most other people would have run away from. His high personal integrity, refined throughout his life, took him from the bottom of the social ladder to the top.

Because of this, Joseph was in a position to help his family and save the young nation of Israel during a time of terrible famine.

Overconfidence without God's perspective will invariably lead us down the pathway to many other personal problems and mistakes. On the other hand, self- assurance linked with a strong faith in God will enable us to overcome the many obstacles we face in life.

God has told us that nothing happens or comes to us that has not passed through his hand first. If He allows things that we think are wrong or that we don't deserve, just stay the course and see how he uses the bad to bring good. Maybe we are learning lessons in how to relate to others problems and help them through or teaching us a lesson. We need to remember whatever he allows in the life of his children is not wasted. "Count it all joy!"

Personally, Joseph's treatment to his brothers and family after all the bad things they did to him, shows him to be a true son of God. First they put him in a pit, took his "coat" and told the father that Joseph was dead. Then they sold him into slavery. He served Potifor and then was imprisoned by a false accusation which put him in a position to interpret dreams of Pharoah's servants. He proved that "prison walls do not a prison make." He acknowledged that his dependence upon God for illumination, proved that he was not a mere dreamer, but an interpreter of dreams, filial devotion and utter submission to God. He knew how to return good for evil. This resulted in Joseph being made the greatest in Egypt, putting him in position to help his family and save the nation of Israel during a time of terrible famine. He also was able to have a reconciliation with brothers by selling them grain and accepting them. We may not be able to arrive at his greatness, but we can emulate his goodness. Joseph later brought his father and His brothers to Egypt and later became the twelve tribes of Judah...Now that is what I call reconciliation!

We need to remember that we are all brothers and sisters in Christ...that makes us family. We need to take a page out of Joseph's book and always love on another, forgiving mistakes, and realizing that all of us are always in need of acceptance and forgiveness. We have it from our Heavenly Father, Jesus paid the price, so let's do the family thing and make Him proud. See you all at the table!

CHAPTER TEN

SUNBATHING TIPS FROM BATHSHEBA

Have you ever noticed how all humans love to point out the mistakes of others. We seem to thrive on the negative acts and allow those to form our opinion of others. If they have done something we think is wrong, then we tend to limit the potential for good in their lives. Take for instance, David and Bathsheba. What we like to remember is that Bathsheba made David sin. Really!! Let's take another look at this situation.

Bathsheba was married to Uriah who was one of David's top soldiers on the battlefield that David had just come home from, because he was tired. Now Bathsheba and Uriah lived in the neighborhood of the palace. Bathsheba was taking a bath in her yard as was the custom of the day. Now David had laid down out on his balcony to rest and was taken aback by Bathsheba's beauty. He sent for her to come to the palace. When she arrived they had a sexual engagement after which, Bathsheba returned home. In due time, she discovered she was pregnant and informed David. David then did the gentlemanly thing and ordered Uriah home from battle. His plan was for the couple to have sex, then they could pass the baby off as the child of Uriah. But...Uriah, being the better man at the moment refused to sleep with his wife while his fellow soldiers were engaged in battle. So he returned to the battlefield. David, not to be outdone, ordered his other officers to arrange the situation so that Uriah would be killed in battle.

Thus for David lust, adultery, deceit, treachery and murder followed in quick succession. Isn't that always the case, one sin leads to another when not confessed.

So after Uriah's death, David had Bathsheba come and live at the palace. She became his wife and their child of an adulterous union was born without disgrace, only to die within a week of his birth. David, mourning over his dead child said, "Can I bring him back again?" " I shall go to him, but he will never return to me."

But what about Bathsheba? Did she also mourn? Did her tears of repentance mingle with those of David. It would seem so, because God blessed them with another son, Solomon, meaning "Beloved of the Lord"

Was this son not an evidence and expression of God's pardoning love for them both? Then remember, that Bathsheba is also included in the genealogy of Jesus another token that God had put her sins behind His back and restored her to divine favor and now virtuous and wise as well as beautiful.

Bathsheba brought up her son Solomon in all godly diligence and care. Solomon himself, came to write, "Train up a child in the way he should go and when he is old, he will not depart from it."

Many have said that it was his mother that Solomon was thinking about when he wrote Proverbs 31 that is now called the story of a virtuous woman. Every preacher who is called upon to do the service for a woman they don't know will almost with out fail, use Proverbs 31 as their text for the service.

So before we are too harsh in our judgment of others, let's take a look in our own lives and experiences. Ever needed a little Forgiveness? Compassion? Love God?

Remember, God always looks down, shakes His head and says, "I already paid for that one too!" We need to accept His forgiveness, not make the same mistakes, and give others the same grace that God gives each of us. Reach out and take the hands of others and say, "God loves you and so do I" Let's learn from our mistakes and not take His grace as weakness or condoning, but rather learn from the experiences and not repeat our mistakes, but repent and live for God!